FIGHT FOR FREEDOM

Contents

Steck Vaughn™

A Harcourt Achieve Imprint

www.Steck-Vaughn.com
1-800-531-5015

T3-BPD-765

What if, like me, you lived during the time of slavery? What would it be like having everything stripped away, including your freedom? My name is Kinna. I was kidnapped from my African home. I was forced aboard a ship to be sold as a slave. But, we didn't give up.

Here are some ideas that will help you understand what happened.

Big Ideas

- Many Africans were captured on the west coast of Africa for slave labor on large farms.

- More than 10 million enslaved Africans were sent to America between 1500 and 1860.

- The route of the slave ships across the Atlantic Ocean was known as the Middle Passage. Many Africans died during this journey.

- Many captured Africans resisted, but few escaped.

- In 1863, President Abraham Lincoln issued the Emancipation Proclamation, freeing all slaves in the South.

Imagine you lived through what I experienced. How would you survive? How important would freedom be to you? As you'll see, I had lots of hardships on my long journey.

Here are some words you'll want to know before reading about my struggle for freedom.

Vocabulary

describe to tell or write about something
*Please **describe** what happened.*

discrimination prejudiced treatment or action against someone by others
*Many people suffer **discrimination** in the world.*

emphasize to highlight or make a point about something
*You can **emphasize** a word in the story by underlining it.*

equality fair or equal treatment for everyone
***Equality** is one of the basic values of the American people.*

justice the upholding of equal rights for all persons under the law
*The victim found **justice** when his attacker went to prison.*

Characters

Kinna,
a member of
the *Amistad* mutiny

Sengbe,
the leader of the mutiny
on the *Amistad*

Keme,
a member of
the *Amistad* mutiny

Jose Ruiz,
a slave trader

Pedro Montes,
a slave trader

John Quincy Adams,
lawyer and
former president

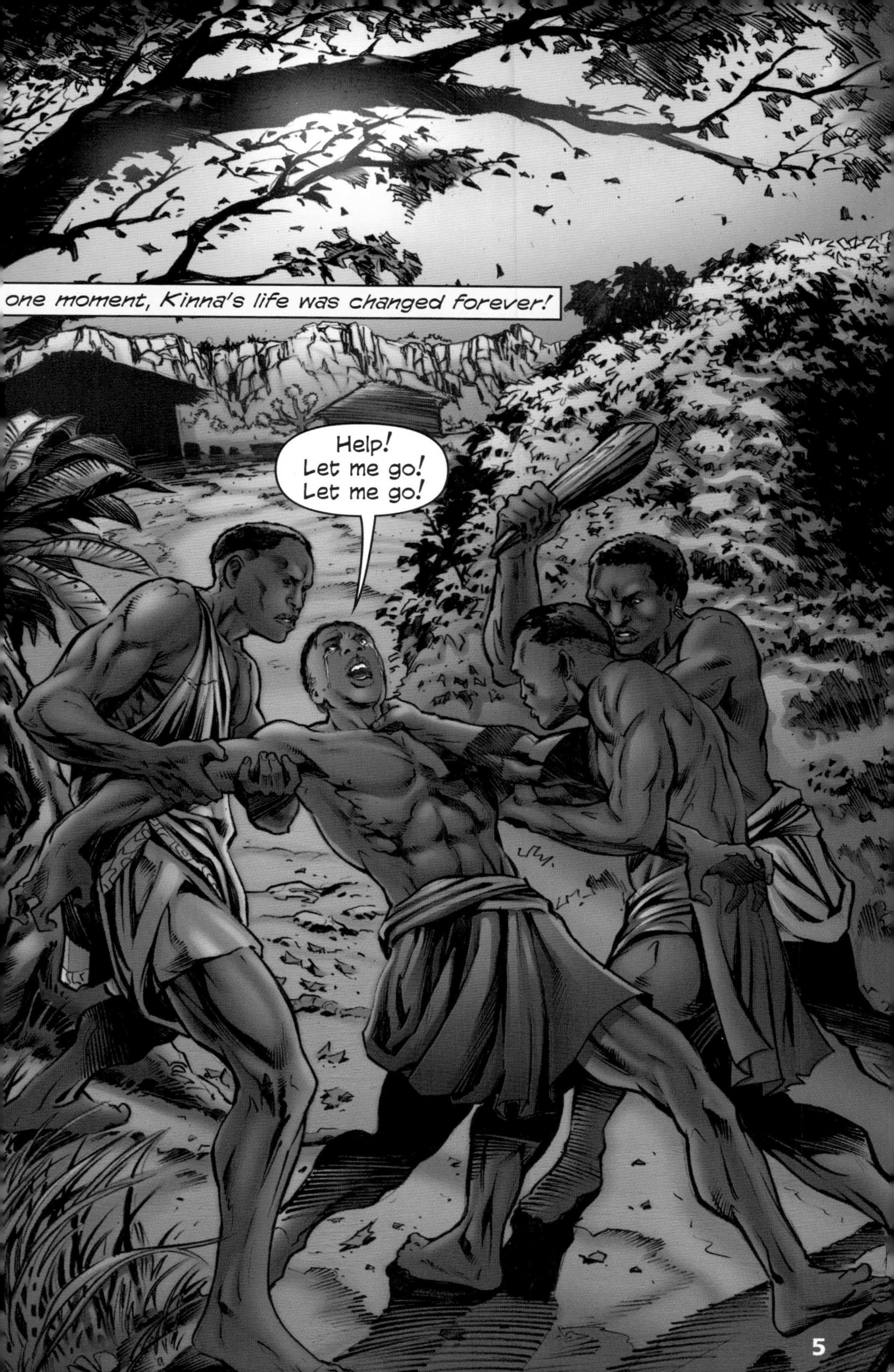
one moment, Kinna's life was changed forever!
Help! Let me go! Let me go!

In 1839, the Mende people lived in small villages in West Africa. Most led peaceful lives farming and going to market. They followed *traditions* handed down over generations.

Don't worry, Mother. I'll be careful.

Sell this cloth at the market. But be careful! There are slave traders around.

Sometimes people were kidnapped and sold as slaves.

Help! Let me go

If you don't keep walking, I will beat you!

Kinna was brought to the coast an put into a *barracoon*, or slave fort

He knew the only way to survive was to find friends who spoke Mende.

Ba-la? Friend?

I am Sengbe. This is Keme.

I am Kinna!

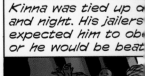

Kinna was tied up a and night. His jailers expected him to ob or he would be beat

Kinna was kept in the barracoon for two months. Then a strange ship arrived.

Tecora

What's that ship?

It's a slave ship. We're going to be sold across the ocean.

Now he knew he would never see his family again.

Come on. Move it!

Would life aboard the ship be any better? He didn't think it could get any worse.

He was wrong.

No, stop!

Words cannot **describe** the **suffering** on the slave ship. Kinna was chained in a space too small to stand. He was starved and beaten.

Kinna, the only way to *survive* this *situation* is to think about other things. Think about being home in Mendeland.

My mother would be making dinner, and...I can't do this!

Once a day, the captives were allowed on deck.

I know I'm still alive as long as I can feel the breeze on my face.

I wish I were strong like you.

I don't know how much longer I can go on.

This trip will be over so my friend.

Not all the captives would be sold as slaves. For many, the slave ship was their last stop.

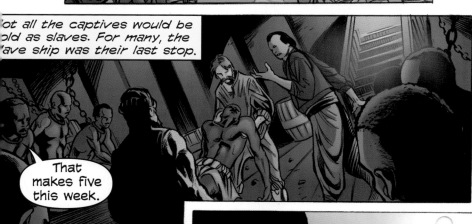

This trip was called the Middle Passage. Millions of Africans were brought across the Atlantic this way. Millions more didn't finish the journey.

After many weeks, the ship finally reached Cuba.

In Havana, Cuba's capital, the Africans were taken off the ship.

Where are we going?

I don't know. Just stay close to me, okay?

They were held in a jail until they could be sold.

Days later, they were taken to the slave market.

These people look at us like we're animals. How can peop treat other human bein this way?

Ah, Jose Ruiz! See anything you like?

These two look strong.

Are you healthy? Open your mouth!

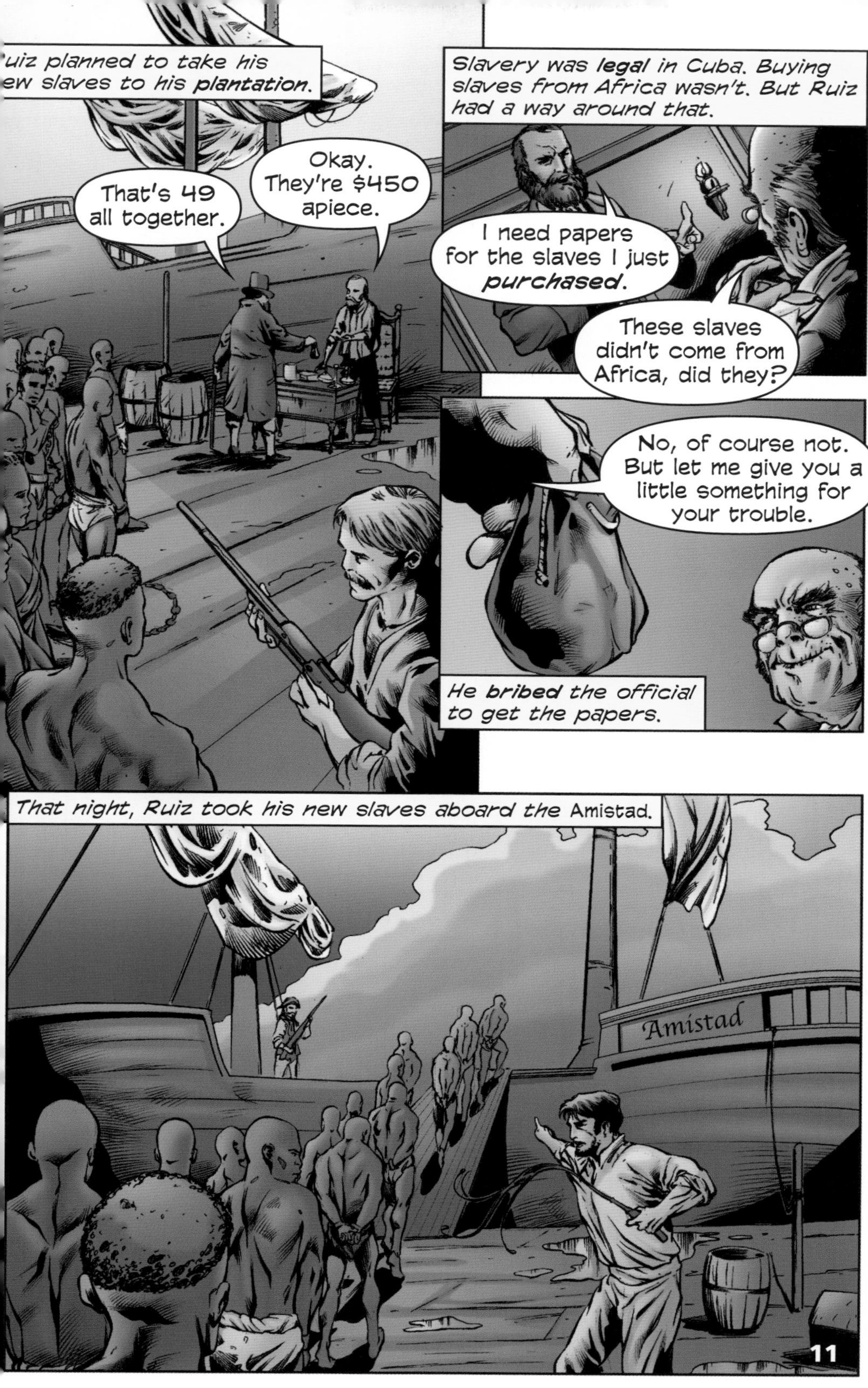
uiz planned to take his
ew slaves to his plantation.
That's 49 all together.
Okay. They're $450 apiece.
Slavery was legal in Cuba. Buying slaves from Africa wasn't. But Ruiz had a way around that.
I need papers for the slaves I just purchased.
These slaves didn't come from Africa, did they?
No, of course not. But let me give you a little something for your trouble.
He bribed the official to get the papers.
That night, Ruiz took his new slaves aboard the Amistad.
Amistad

This time, it was Kinna who had to comfort Sengbe.

Not this again! I won't be chained up. I'll escape!

We survived it before. We can do it again if we stick together.

The trip was only supposed to take a few days. But things went horribly wrong.

This slave stole water. Have him whipped. Then rub salt in the wounds.

Meanwhile, below deck, Sengbe had plans of his own.

Do these men treat us with *equality* and *respect*? No, they treat us like animals. We must escape.

How?

With this!

That night, Sengbe used the nail to free himself and the rest of the Africans.

Quick! Me next!

Here, take these *machetes*. We might need them.

They went up on deck. Surprise was on their side.

In a matter of minutes, it was all over. The Africans had taken control of the Amistad.

Stop! Help!

13

Some sailors fled in a lifeboat. But Ruiz and Pedro Montes were kept as prisoners. The Africans needed them to sail the ship.

Take this ship back to Africa. We want to go home.

Each morning they made Ruiz head east, into the rising sun. That was the way back to Africa.

When night fell, it was impossible to tell which way the ship was going. Montes and Ruiz would turn around and head west.

The *Amistad* traveled this way for weeks. Some Africans began to starve and get sick.

The ship wasn't stocked for such a long trip. We're running low on food and water.

We don't have enough supplies to reach Africa.

e Amistad *attracted*
ot of **attention**.
ople on other ships
ndered about the
range ship full
Africans. Some
ught it should
captured.

Weird Ship

ispicious Sail— A Pirate

The Spanish Slaver

The Amistad
had sailed
all the way
north to
Long Island,
New York.

One morning, Sengbe went ashore to buy food and water.

While they were gone, a ship pulled up alongside the Amistad and captured it.

Prepare to be boarded!

The men on shore were captured as well. The Amistad's long journey was over.

15

The Africans were taken to a jail in New Haven, Connecticut. But Ruiz claimed the slaves were his property and should go back to Cuba.

In chains again! Is there no *justice* in life?

Many people in the U.S. were against slavery. These **abolitionists** didn't want the Africans sent back to Cuba.

We know you come from Africa and are not slaves. We want to help. But we need some *information*.

We must find someone who speaks your language. Teach us to count to ten.

The abolitionists went down to the docks and began counting in Mende.

E-ta, fe-le, sau-wa.

They found a British sailor who was from Mendeland.

Excuse me, are you speaking Mende?

Through the *translator*, Sengbe told the story of how the Africans came to be aboard the Amistad.

No one could agree on what to do with the Africans. The case ended up in court. Ruiz wanted the court to *declare* that the Africans were slaves. The abolitionists wanted the court to say that they weren't.

...awyer named Roger Baldwin ...resented the Africans.

These people were brought to Cuba from Africa. Since it's *illegal* to bring slaves from Africa, I must *emphasize* that these people can't be slaves.

...t Sengbe had no patience ... the court. If they were ...ught from Africa illegally, ...y couldn't they just be ... free?

Give us freedom! Give us freedom!

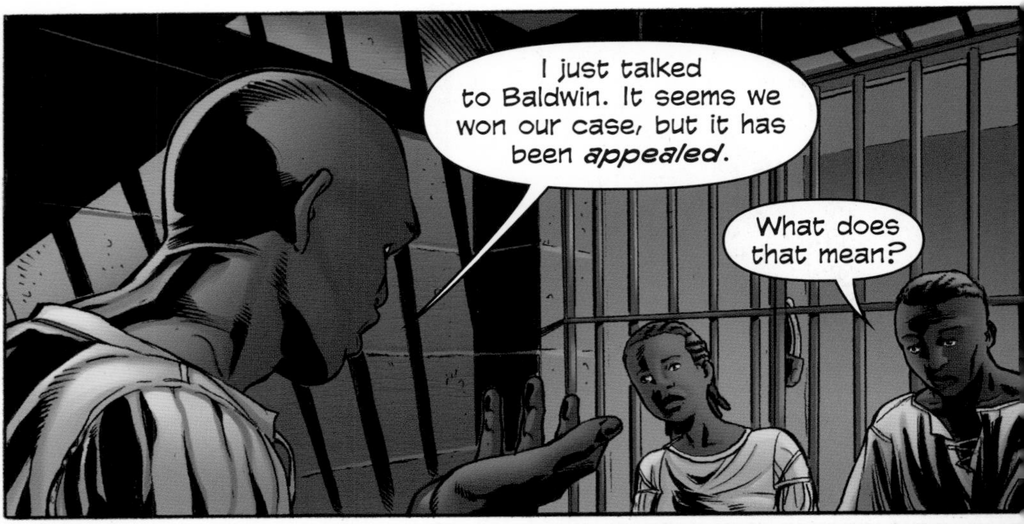
I just talked to Baldwin. It seems we won our case, but it has been *appealed*.
What does that mean?

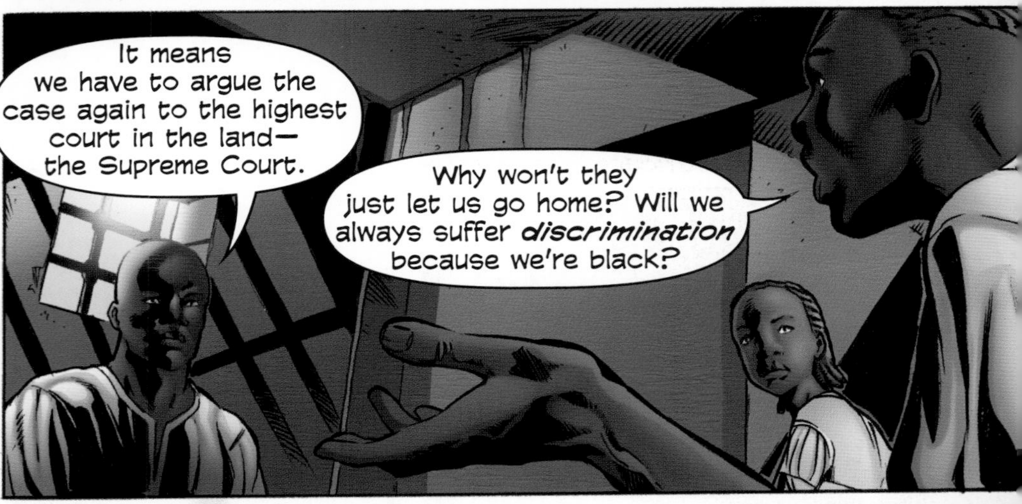
It means we have to argue the case again to the highest court in the land—the Supreme Court.
Why won't they just let us go home? Will we always suffer *discrimination* because we're black?

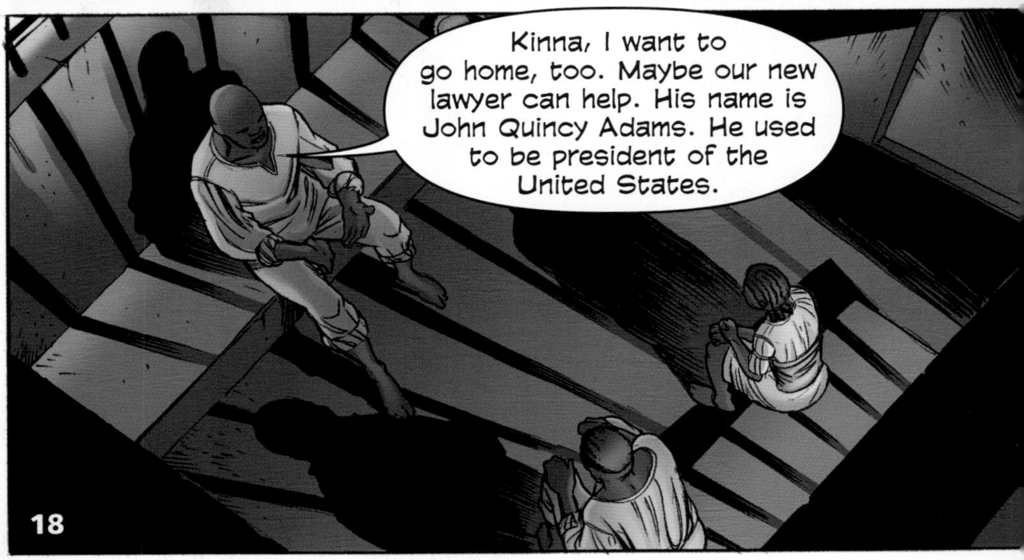
Kinna, I want to go home, too. Maybe our new lawyer can help. His name is John Quincy Adams. He used to be president of the United States.

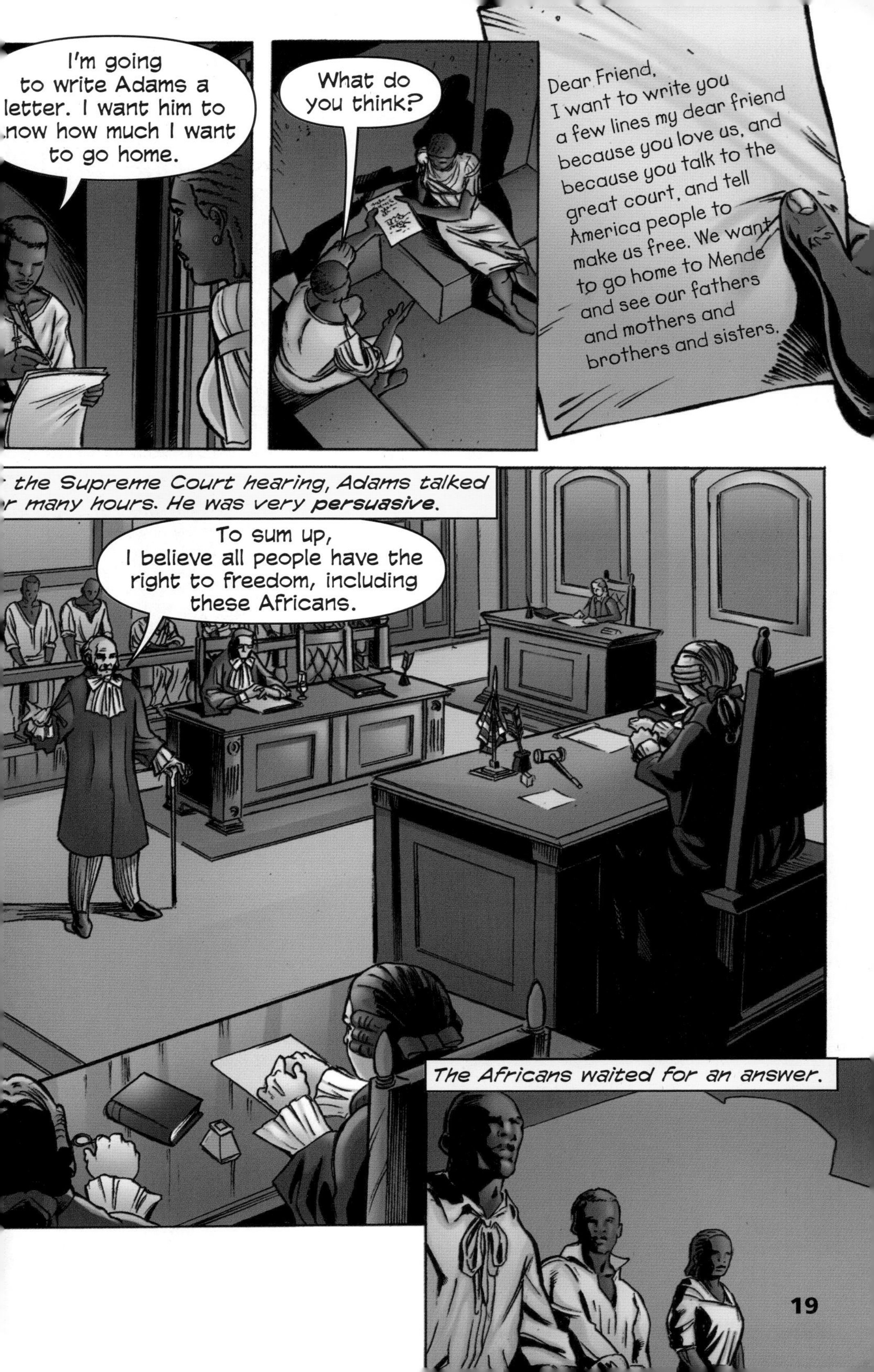

I'm going to write Adams a letter. I want him to now how much I want to go home.
What do you think?
Dear Friend, I want to write you a few lines my dear friend because you love us, and because you talk to the great court, and tell America people to make us free. We want to go home to Mende and see our fathers and mothers and brothers and sisters.
the Supreme Court hearing, Adams talked r many hours. He was very **persuasive**.
To sum up, I believe all people have the right to freedom, including these Africans.
The Africans waited for an answer.

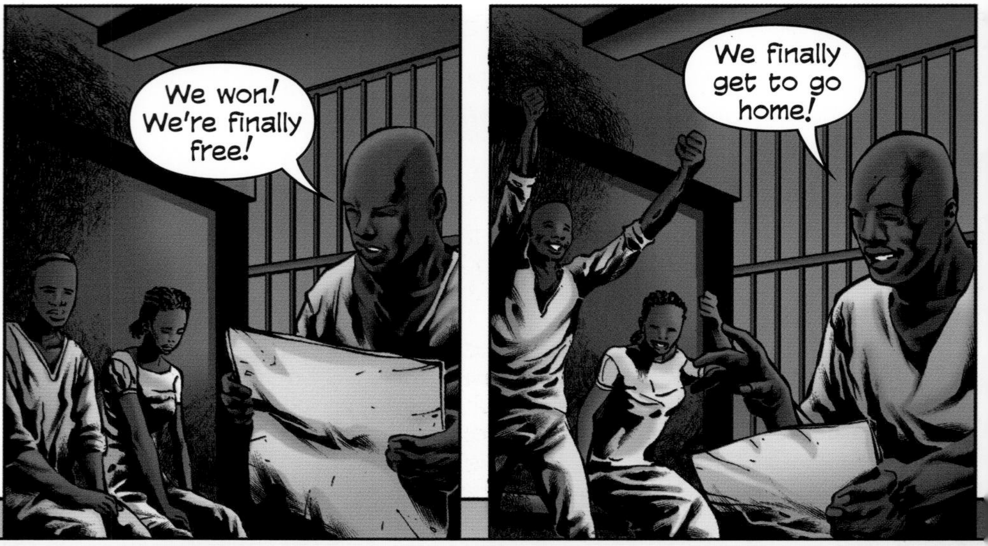
We won! We're finally free!
We finally get to go home!

It took another seven months, but the Amistad *Africans finally sailed for home. In November of 1841, the ship* Gentleman *set sail for Africa. Kinna, Keme, and Sengbe were on their way back to Africa at last.*

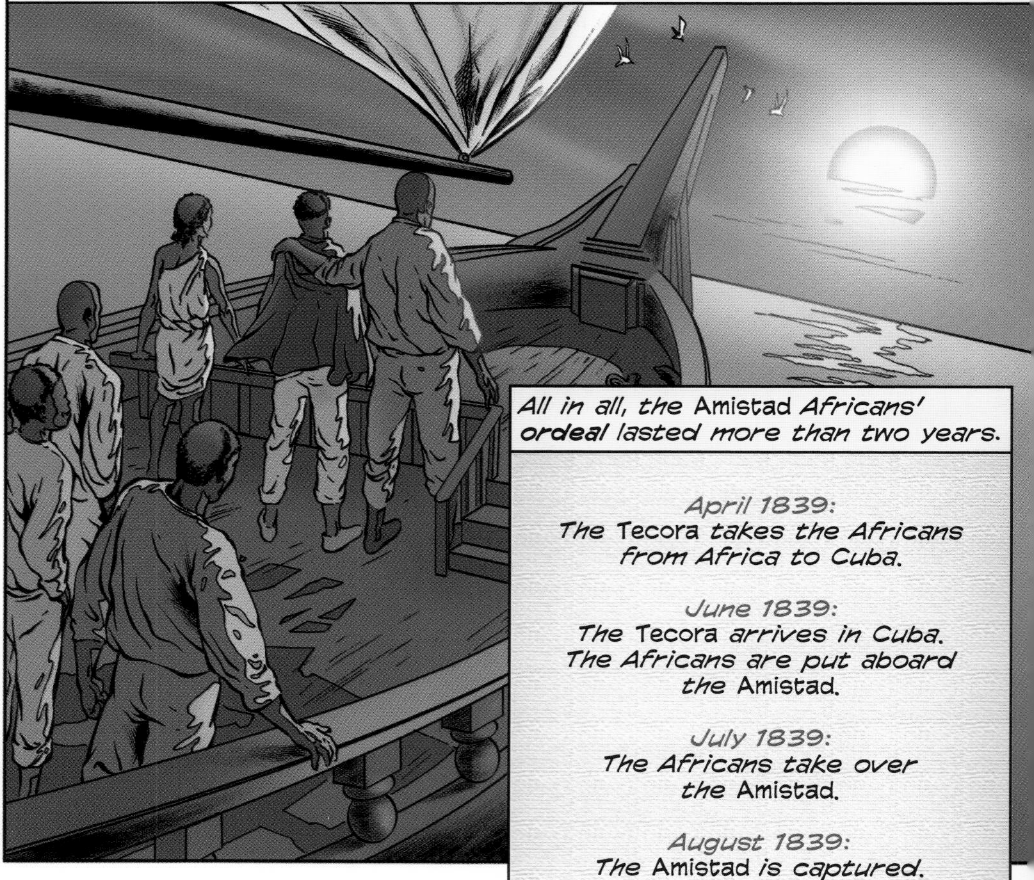

All in all, the Amistad *Africans' **ordeal** lasted more than two years.*

April 1839:
The Tecora *takes the Africans from Africa to Cuba.*

June 1839:
The Tecora *arrives in Cuba. The Africans are put aboard the* Amistad.

July 1839:
The Africans take over the Amistad.

August 1839:
The Amistad *is captured.*

November 1841:
35 Amistad *Africans sail home.*

Wrap Up

Aboard the *Amistad*, we never stopped thinking about our freedom. We risked our lives for it. Over the course of many years, millions of Africans were enslaved and forced aboard ships like the *Amistad*. Many died during the Middle Passage to America. Those who survived passed the hope for freedom down through the years. Finally, in 1863, President Lincoln freed the slaves in the South.

What rights do free people have? How do we make sure those rights are protected?

Find out in *Voices of Freedom: Civil Rights in the United States and South Africa*.

Voices of Freedom

Civil Rights in the United States and South Africa

Jackie Glasthal

Glossary

abolitionist (*noun*) someone who fights against slavery

appeal (*verb*) to request a new trial once a judge has ruled

attention (*noun*) notice; consideration

barracoon (*noun*) a jail or fort for slaves

bribe (*verb*) to offer or give money in exchange for special favors

declare (*verb*) to state or say something

describe (*verb*) to tell or write about something

discrimination (*noun*) prejudiced treatment or action against someone by others

emphasize (*verb*) to highlight or make a point about something

equality (*noun*) fair or equal treatment for everyone

illegal (*adjective*) against the law

information (*noun*) a collection of facts; knowledge

justice (*noun*) the upholding of equal rights for all persons under the law

legal (*adjective*) within the limits of the law

machete (*noun*) a large knife

Middle Passage (*noun*) the route of slave trading ships from Africa to the West Indies

ordeal (*noun*) a difficult event that happens to someone

persuasive (*adjective*) having the ability to change someone's opinion or point of view

plantation (*noun*) a large farm with crops raised by many workers

purchase (*verb*) to buy

respect (*noun*) high regard or appreciation

situation (*noun*) the circumstances at a given moment

suffering (*noun*) a time of pain or hurt

survive (*verb*) to remain alive through a hardship

tradition (*noun*) a long-standing action or routine that is taught or handed down to others

translator (*noun*) an interpreter; someone who translates one language into another language

Idioms

stick together (*page 12*) to support or stay close to someone
We will stick together and help each other through this problem.

surprise was on their side (*page 13*) the edge or benefit of catching someone unprepared
When the soldiers attacked the enemy, surprise was on their side.